LAYING FLOORS

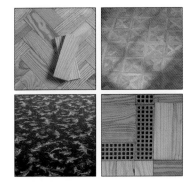

LAYING FLOORS

Mike Lawrence

LORENZ BOOKS

This edition is published by Lorenz Books,
an imprint of Anness Publishing Ltd,
Blaby Road,
Wigston,
Leicestershire LE18 4SE;

info@anness.com

www.lorenzbooks.com;
www.annesspublishing.com

If you like the images in this book
and would like to investigate using
them for publishing, promotions or
advertising, please visit our website
www.practicalpictures.com
for more information.

Publisher: Joanna Lorenz
Editors: Felicity Forster, Anne Hildyard
Photographer: John Freeman
Illustrator: Andrew Green
Designer: Bill Mason
Production Controller: Pirong Wang

Additional text: Catherine Tully

ACKNOWLEDGEMENTS AND NOTES
The publisher would like to
thank The Tool Shop for supplying
tools for jacket photography:
97 Lower Marsh
Waterloo, London SE1 7AB
Tel 020 7207 2077; Fax 020 7207 5222
www.thetoolshop-diy.com

The author and publishers have made
every effort to ensure that all instructions
contained within this book are accurate
and safe, and cannot accept liability for
any resulting injury, damage or loss to
persons or property, however it may arise.
If in any doubt as to the correct procedure
to follow for any home improvements
task, seek professional advice.

CONTENTS

INTRODUCTION

The wide range of floor coverings available to choose from includes decorative wood panels and strips, sheet vinyl and carpets.

There are two main types of wooden floor covering: wood-block, sometimes called wood mosaic, and woodstrip. The former consists of small slivers of wood (usually a hardwood) laid in groups and stuck to strong cloth to form wooden "tiles", while the latter is just what its name implies: narrow hardwood planks laid over an existing floor.

Sheet vinyl floor coverings come in a huge range of colours and patterns, and may also have a surface embossed along the lines of the design to give plausible imitations of other floor coverings such as tiles, marble, wood and cork. Some more expensive types have a cushioned underside formed by incorporating small air bubbles during manufacture, which makes them warmer and softer underfoot than their solid counterparts.

Carpets laid loose have been used on floors for millennia, but it was only a few decades ago that wall-to-wall fitted carpeting became popular. Traditional woven carpets made from natural fibres have been challenged by carpets made from synthetic fibres and by alternative methods of manufacture. There is now a huge choice of colours and patterns in types to suit all locations and wear conditions, available in a variety of widths.

While some floor coverings require more skill than others to lay, with care and forethought all can be

LEFT: Subtle variations of colour make wooden floorboards particularly attractive.

ABOVE: Sheet vinyl is durable and easy to clean, and is available in a range of colours and patterns.

BELOW: Carpeting provides luxury underfoot, and it is very comfortable in living rooms.

installed by the determined do-it-yourselfer. Moreover, with a little imagination, many floor coverings can be used to produce eye-catching and unusual effects to match or complement the décor of a room.

Remember that practicality is important when choosing a floor covering. Always consider whether the area to be covered will be exposed to water, as in a bathroom, or to heavy wear, as in a kitchen, and whether durability is paramount or a more whimsical surface would suffice. Above all, choose projects that appeal to you and that will produce floors you will enjoy creating and living with.

MATERIALS & EQUIPMENT

When choosing new floor coverings, remember that there is more to it than simply ordering wall-to-wall carpet throughout, and mistakes can be expensive. Floor coverings have to withstand a great deal of wear and tear in certain areas of the average home, especially if there are children or pets in the family, so choosing the right material is very important. Luckily, there is a wide choice of materials, and laying them is well within the capability of most people. Shopping for floor coverings has never been easier either. All the major do-it-yourself suppliers stock a huge range of materials – plus all the tools needed to lay them. If they do not stock what you need, try specialist flooring and carpet suppliers.

WOOD FLOOR COVERINGS

These come in two main forms: as square wood-block panels made up of individual fingers of wood stuck to a cloth or felt backing for ease of handling and laying; or as woodstrip flooring – interlocking planks, often of veneer on a plywood backing. They are laid over the existing floor surface. Most are tongued-and-grooved, so only occasional nailing or clipping is required to hold them in place.

Wood-block panels are usually 300 or 450mm (12 or 18in) square, while planks are generally 75 or 100mm (3 or 4in) wide and come in a range of lengths to allow the end joints to be staggered from one row to the next so that they all line up.

LEFT: Wooden flooring materials can be used like tiles, creating a combination of interlocking shapes and natural textures.

BELOW: Parquet is created by laying blocks of wood in a variety of geometric patterns.

ABOVE: Give a contemporary interpretation to traditional parquet flooring by colourwashing the blocks. This provides a subtle means of matching the floor to your decorative scheme.

RIGHT: Hard-wearing and elegant, woodstrip flooring is a practical choice for living rooms and hallways.

FAR RIGHT: Wood squares can be painted in alternate colours, creating a chequerboard design. It is also possible to combine different wood effects, such as walnut and maple.

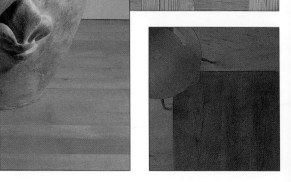

VINYL, LINOLEUM AND CORK

Vinyl is available as sheets and tiles. Sheet vinyl is a relatively thin material that provides a smooth, hygienic and easy-to-clean floor covering, which is widely used in rooms such as kitchens, bathrooms and hallways. It is made from layers of plastic resin, with a clear wear layer protecting the printed design and frequently an air-cushion layer between this and the backing for extra comfort and warmth underfoot. Vinyl tiles come in a wide range of plain and patterned types, and are laid with double-sided adhesive.

Linoleum (lino) is becoming popular again for domestic use, and is also available in sheet form and as tiles, in some stylish designs and colourways with optional contrasting border designs. Lino is more difficult for the amateur to lay, however, being heavier, less flexible and harder to cut than vinyl.

ABOVE: Vinyl flooring is available in a wide range of decorative designs, including realistic imitations of ceramic tiles, wood panels, cork tiles and stone. The covering shown here is imitating an intricate wooden pattern.

Cork is frequently used in work areas such as kitchens and bathrooms. It offers a unique combination of warmth and resilience underfoot, coupled with an easy-to-clean surface that looks attractive too.

ABOVE: Sheet vinyl can offer excellent imitations of a wide range of other floor coverings, including marble, terrazzo and, shown here, woodstrip.

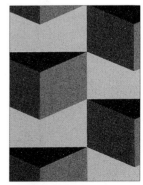

ABOVE: Linoleum shapes can be cut and adhered to the floor to produce patterns. Lino is ideal for kitchens, with its hard-wearing, easy-to-clean surface.

CARPETS

Carpets consist of fibre tufts or loops woven or stuck to a durable backing. Woven carpets are generally the most expensive. Modern types are made by either the Axminster or the Wilton method, which differ in technical details, but both produce a durable product that can be either patterned or plain. Tufted carpets are made by stitching tufts of fibre into a woven backing, where they are secured by attaching a second backing under the first with adhesive. Some of the less expensive types have a foam underlay bonded directly to the backing; others require a separate underlay to be laid.

A wide range of fibre types is used in carpet construction, including wool, nylon, acrylic, polypropylene and viscose rayon, as well as modern natural materials such as coir, sisal and seagrass. Fibre blends can improve carpet performance; a mixture of 80 per cent wool and 20 per cent nylon is particularly popular for providing a combination of warmth, resilience, low flammability and resistance to soiling.

Pile length and density affect the carpet's performance as well as its looks, and most carpets are classified to indicate the sort of wear they can be expected to withstand. The pile can be cut, often to different lengths, giving a sculptured effect; looped (shag), that is, uncut and left long; corded, which means uncut and pulled tight to the backing; or twisted, which gives a tufty effect. A dense pile wears better than a loosely woven one, which can be parted to reveal the backing.

Carpet widths are described as broadloom, more than 1.8m (6ft) wide; or body (stair carpet), usually up to 900mm (3ft) wide. The former are intended for large areas, the latter for corridors and stairs. Broadloom carpet is available in various metric and imperial widths.

ABOVE AND LEFT: The range of colours and patterns of carpet available makes it possible to complement and enhance any style of interior. Carpets are made in qualities to match the requirements of every room in the house.

CARPET TILES

These are small squares of carpet of various types, designed to be loose-laid. Cheaper tiles resemble cord and felt carpets, while more expensive ones may have a short or long cut pile. Common sizes are 300, 450, 500 and 600mm (12, 18, 20 and 24in) square.

Along with lino tiles, carpet tiles are real winners in the practicality stakes. Almost unbeatable in areas that need to be hard-wearing and where children and their attendant wear and tear are concerned, carpet tiles have the single disadvantage that they never look like fitted carpet, no matter how well they are laid. Rather than fighting the fact that they come in non-fraying squares, make use of this very quality and create a fun floor-scape, such as a giant board game. Carpet tiles are very forgiving, allowing for slight discrepancies in cutting, and are very easy to replace if an area is damaged. A geometrical design is easiest; it is advisable to leave curves to the experts, but anything else – even the elegance of a painting by Mondrian – is possible.

ABOVE: Carpet tiles have a long commercial pedigree, and can be a clever choice in the home too, since they can be lifted for cleaning and rotated to even out the effects of wear.

LEFT: Small carpet tiles can be used to create intricate patterns, such as this large backgammon board game. Such patterns need working out carefully on paper first and can be fiddly to lay, but the finished effect is well worth the effort.

MATERIALS FOR DIFFERENT ROOMS

I n principle, it is possible to lay any floor covering in any room of a home. However, custom and the practicalities of life tend to divide the home into three broad areas.

Access areas, such as halls, landings and stairs, need a floor covering that is able to cope with heavy traffic and muddy shoes. Ideal choices for hallways are materials with a water-repellent and easy-clean surface – for example, sheet vinyl, vinyl tiles, a woodstrip or wood-block floor, sanded and sealed floorboards, or glazed ceramic or quarry tiles. For stairs, where safety is paramount, the best material to choose is a heavy-duty carpet with a short pile, which can also be used on landings.

Work areas, such as kitchens and bathrooms, also need durable floor coverings that are easy to clean and, especially in the case of bathrooms,

ABOVE: Plain carpets are the key to simple, yet sophisticated, colour schemes. Neutral tones can be offset with the subtlest of colour contrasts.

LEFT: Cork is the warmest of tiled floor coverings underfoot, and when sealed is good-looking and durable too.

water-resistant as well. Sheet vinyl is a popular choice for both rooms, but tiles of various types can also provide an excellent surface – sealed cork, with its warm feel underfoot, is particularly suitable in bathrooms. However, if carpet is preferred for these rooms, there are extremely hard-wearing kitchen carpets available, with a specially treated short nylon pile that is easy to keep clean, and also

RIGHT: Solid woodstrip flooring, shown here in beech, provides a luxury floor covering that looks stunning and will also last for a lifetime.

water-resistant bathroom carpets that give a touch of luxury underfoot without turning into a swamp at bath time.

Leisure areas – living rooms, dining rooms and bedrooms – are commonly carpeted wall to wall. Do not be tempted to skimp on quality in living rooms, which receive the most wear and tend to develop distinct traffic routes. However, it is reasonable to choose light-duty types for bedrooms.

Alternatives to carpets depend simply on taste in home décor. Options include sanded and sealed floorboards teamed with scatter rugs, or a parquet perimeter to a fine specimen carpet. Woodstrip, sheet vinyl or cork tiles may also be worth considering for children's rooms.

ABOVE: Wood is an excellent choice for entrance halls too, where a durable, yet good-looking, floor surface is essential.

TOOLS FOR WOOD AND VINYL

For laying wood-block and woodstrip floor coverings, you will need general woodworking tools, adhesive and a spreader for wood-block floors, and pins (tacks) or fixing clips for woodstrip floors, plus varnish or sealer if laying an unsealed type. For marking out, you will require a retractable steel tape measure, a pencil and a straightedge. Wooden blocks and strips can be cut to length with a tenon saw, while cut-outs can be made in them to fit around obstacles with a coping saw, pad saw or electric jigsaw (saber saw).

For laying sheet vinyl, a tape measure and sharp utility knife are needed. A long steel straightedge will also be invaluable. For bonding the lengths to the floor along edges and seams, use either double-sided adhesive tape or bands of liquid adhesive, spread with a toothed spreader to ensure that a uniform amount of adhesive is applied.

Lastly, for both wooden and vinyl floor coverings you will need a pair of compasses or a scribing block and pencil, plus a shape tracer with adjustable steel or plastic fingers, to transfer the outlines of the various floor-level obstacles along the edges of the room so that they can be trimmed to fit around them.

Unless they are to be continued into an adjoining room, both types of flooring will need finishing off at doorways, This is achieved by fitting ready-made threshold (saddle) strips.

threshold (saddle) cover strip

staples

staple hammer

coping saw

tenon saw

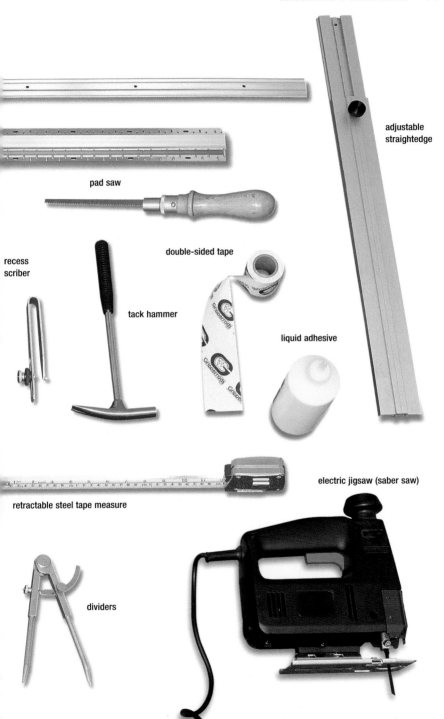

adjustable
straightedge

pad saw

recess
scriber

double-sided tape

tack hammer

liquid adhesive

retractable steel tape measure

electric jigsaw (saber saw)

dividers

TOOLS FOR LAYING CARPET

For laying carpet, the basic essentials are a tape measure and a sharp utility knife. As an alternative, special carpet shears can be used.

For a woven carpet, a carpet stretcher is invaluable. This is a device with a horizontal pad of metal spikes at one end, which is locked into the carpet, and a cushioned pad at the other end, which is nudged with the knee to stretch the carpet into place. It is probably best to hire this tool.

Also needed are some carpet gripper strips to hold the carpet in position around the perimeter of the room. These are thin strips of plywood fitted with angled nails that grip the underside of the carpet, and are nailed to the floor about 10mm (⅜in) from the skirting (baseboard). The edge of the carpet is tucked down into the gap, usually with a carpet fitter's bolster. A wide brick bolster (stonecutter's chisel) may be used, as long as it is clean.

Foam-backed carpet may be stapled to the floor or stuck down with double-sided adhesive tape. Adhesive seaming tape may also be needed to join sections of carpet together, and threshold (saddle) strips are used to trim the carpeted edge off at door openings.

Lining paper or cloth underlay is recommended for foam-backed carpets, as it prevents the foam from sticking to the floor surface. For woven carpets, use either a foam or felt underlay: they are available in various grades and should be matched to the carpet.

gripper strips

carpet knife with spare blades

left-handed carpet shears

staples

staple hammer

hessian (burlap) carpet tape

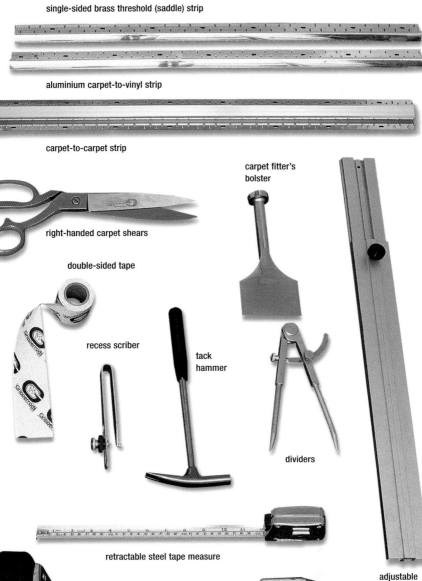

single-sided brass threshold (saddle) strip

aluminium carpet-to-vinyl strip

carpet-to-carpet strip

carpet fitter's bolster

right-handed carpet shears

double-sided tape

recess scriber

tack hammer

dividers

adjustable straightedge

retractable steel tape measure

carpet stretcher

PREPARATION

All floor coverings must be laid on a sound, flat surface. With a wooden structure, the older the floor, the more likely it is that there will be loose or damaged boards, or protruding nail heads. With a concrete floor there may be cracks, an uneven surface or, worse, damp patches. All of these conditions must be rectified before laying your new floor covering. If wooden boards are in reasonable condition, they may need only sanding to remove high spots; otherwise, they can be covered with sheets of hardboard, plywood or chipboard (particle board). Concrete can also be covered in this manner or finished with a self-levelling floor screed. If you are in any doubt about your ability in this respect, seek professional help.

REMOVING OLD FLOOR COVERINGS

Generally speaking, old floor coverings should always be lifted before laying new ones. This also provides an opportunity to inspect the floor itself and to carry out any repairs that may be necessary. However, there are some situations where it may not be practical or necessary to lift an existing floor covering – for example, where vinyl tiles have been laid over a concrete floor and they are firmly stuck to it. Stripping such a large area will be an extremely time-consuming job unless a professional floor tile stripping machine is hired.

Wood-block or woodstrip floors should be lifted if damaged or loose, otherwise cover them by pinning on hardboard sheets.

1 The backing of old foam-backed carpets may remain stuck to the floor surface after the carpet has lifted. Scrape and brush it up, and also remove any remaining staples and remnants of seaming tape.

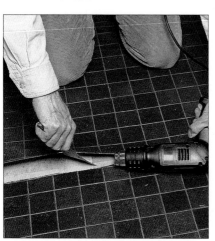

2 To lift vinyl tiles or sheet vinyl that has been stuck along edges and seams, use a heat gun to soften the adhesive and quickly pull up the flooring. Work the blade of a scraper beneath the edges so that you can lift them.

3 If vinyl or cork tiles have been stuck on to a hardboard underlay, lift a few tiles to expose the board edges, then lever up the boards in one piece.

RENOVATING FLOOR BOARDS

For suspended wood floors – boards laid over floor joists – start by lifting the old floor covering and checking that all the boards are securely fixed to their joists, and that they are reasonably flat and level. Loose boards will creak annoyingly when walked on, and raised edges or pronounced warping may show as distinct lines through the new floor covering.

Use either cut nails or large oval-headed nails to secure loose boards. When driving them near known pipe or cable runs, take care not to pierce them; it is best to drive the new nails as close to existing nail positions as possible for safety. If there are only one or two loose boards, secure them with screws rather than nails.

Another problem with floor boards, particularly if they are very old, is that gaps can open up between them. When laying a flexible floor covering over them, such as carpet or vinyl, the gaps may cause irregularities in the surface, leading to noticeable wear patterns. One solution is to glue strips of wood into the gaps, planing them flush with the boards when the glue has dried. If they are really bad, however, it may be worth lifting all the boards and relaying them, clamping them tightly together as you do so with hired flooring cramps. Any remaining gaps will need filling with a narrow board. Obviously, this is quite a drastic solution, and it may be simpler to clad the floor with hardboard sheets.

1 Drive in any nails that have lifted due to warping or twisting of the floorboards, then recess their heads slightly using a nail punch. If existing nails have pulled through a board, drive in new ones, slightly to one side.

2 If nails will not hold the floorboard flat against the joist, drill pilot and clearance holes, and use wood screws to secure the board firmly in place. Countersink the holes so that the screw heads sit below the surface of the board.

LAYING HARDBOARD

Covering existing floorboards with a hardboard underlay is an alternative to floor sanding as a way of ensuring a smooth, flat surface ideal for thin sheet floor coverings. Lay the boards in rows with the joints staggered from row to row, and pin them down with hardboard pins (tacks) driven in at 150mm (6in) spacings. Lay separate strips above known pipe runs so that you can get to them easily should the need arise.

Before you begin, condition the boards to the temperature and humidity conditions in the room so that they will not become warped after laying. Soak the textured sides of the boards with warm water, then stack them back to back in the room for at least 24 hours. It is best to lay the hardboard textured side uppermost to provide an additional key for the flooring adhesive. In addition, the indentations in the board will accommodate the nail heads, preventing them from damaging the floor covering.

Dry-lay the boards first, working out from the centre of the room and making sure that their edges do not coincide with the gaps between floorboards. Check also that you will not be left with impossibly narrow gaps to fill at the walls. If necessary, shift the position of the first board to one side or the other.

If preparing to lay glazed ceramic or quarry tiles on a suspended wood floor, put down exterior-grade plywood.

1 If hardboard sheets are used as an underlay for a new floor covering, start by punching in any raised nail heads all over the floor.

2 Nail the hardboard sheets to the floorboards at 150mm (6in) intervals along the edges and also 300mm (12in) apart across the face of each sheet. Lay the boards in rows, staggering the joints from one row to the next.

LAYING A CHIPBOARD FLOOR

To level and insulate a concrete floor, you can cover the concrete with a floating floor of chipboard (particle board), if raising the floor level will not cause problems at door thresholds. The chipboard can be laid directly on the concrete over heavy-duty plastic sheeting, which acts as a vapour barrier. If additional insulation is required, put down polystyrene (plastic foam) boards first, then lay the new flooring on top of them.

Treat damp floors with one or two coats of a proprietary damp-proofing liquid and allow to dry before laying the vapour barrier. Widespread rising damp may require more radical treatment, in which case, it is best to seek professional help.

1 Before you begin laying the chipboard (particle board) panels, prepare the floor surface. First, remove the skirtings (baseboards). Next, put down heavy-duty plastic sheets to prevent moisture rising through the floor.

2 Tape the sheets to the walls; they will be hidden behind the skirting later. Then butt-joint 25mm (1in) polystyrene (plastic foam) insulation boards over the floor, staggering the joints in adjacent rows.

3 Cover the insulation with tongued-and-grooved flooring-grade boards. Use cut pieces as necessary, and add a tapered threshold (saddle) strip at the door. When finished, replace the skirtings.

LAYING SELF-SMOOTHING COMPOUND

Ground floors of solid concrete are prone to two main problems: cracking or potholing of the surface, and rising damp caused by a failure in the damp-proof membrane within the floor structure. Cracks and depressions may show through new floor coverings, especially thinner types such as sheet vinyl, while dampness will encourage mould growth beneath the covering, so both these problems must be eradicated before laying a new floor.

Relatively narrow cracks can be patched with either a repair mortar of one part cement to three parts sand or with an exterior-quality masonry filler.

If the floor surface is uneven or pitted, it can be covered with a thin layer of self-smoothing compound. There are two types available; both are powders and are mixed with either water or with a special latex emulsion. The compound is mixed in a bucket and poured on to the floor surface, trowelling it out to a thickness of about 3mm (⅛in). The liquid finds its own level and dries to give a hard, smooth surface that can be walked on in about 1 hour. Leave it to dry for 24 hours before laying a floor covering over it.

At a door opening, it is necessary to nail a thin strip of wood across the threshold to contain the levelling compound and prevent it from spreading beyond the room. Use masonry nails to hold the wood in place, leaving their heads proud so that they can be prised out and the wood removed once the compound has dried.

1 Start by sweeping the floor clear of dust and debris. Then scrub away any patches of grease from the surface with strong detergent solution. Fill any cracks or holes deeper than 3mm (⅛in) with mortar or filler.

4 Mix up the self-smoothing compound in a bucket, following the manufacturer's instructions carefully to ensure that the mix is of the right consistency and free from lumps.

2 Key the surface of vinyl floor tiles by sanding them before laying the compound. Wipe away the dust with a damp cloth.

3 If the concrete surface is very dusty or appears unduly porous, seal it by brushing on a generous coat of PVA building adhesive (white general-purpose adhesive) diluted with about five parts water.

5 Starting in the corner of the room that is farthest from the door, pour the self-smoothing compound on to the floor surface to cover an area of about 1 sq m (11 sq ft).

6 Use a plasterer's trowel to spread the compound out to a thickness of about 3mm (⅛in). Mix, pour and level further batches as required until the entire floor has been covered. Leave to dry for 24 hours.

FLOORING TECHNIQUES

A variety of techniques can be used to give a floor a new lease of life, whether it is simply brightening up an existing boarded floor with a coat of varnish or paint, laying a practical, hard-wearing covering or putting down a thick carpet to provide some underfoot luxury. Always consider the type of wear and tear the flooring will be subjected to and choose appropriately. Take the time to work out the quantities of materials needed – your supplier will often be able to help you in this respect – and make sure that you have everything to hand before you begin work. Clear the room of all furnishings and keep children and pets out of the way until you have finished.

SANDING WOOD FLOORS

Where old floorboards are very uneven, or it is planned to leave them exposed but they are badly stained and marked, you will need to sand them. Hire a floor sanding machine to do this. It resembles a cylinder (reel) lawnmower, with a drum to which sheets of abrasive paper are fitted. A bag at the rear collects the sawdust; however, always wear a face mask and goggles when sanding floors. Also hire a smaller disc or belt sander for finishing off the room edges.

If necessary, drive any visible nail heads below the surface. Start sanding with coarse abrasive paper, running the machine at 45 degrees to the board direction, then use medium and fine paper in turn with the machine running parallel to the boards. Use the disc or belt sander to tackle the perimeter of the room where the large sander cannot reach. Even so, this will not sand right up to the skirtings (baseboards) or into the corners, and the only solution in these areas is to use a hand scraper.

FINISHING

Once the floor has been sanded, sweep up the remaining dust and vacuum the floor. If you intend laying a floor covering, you need do no more. If you want to leave the boards exposed, wipe them with a cloth moistened with white spirit (paint thinner). This will remove any remaining dust.

If you want to make the most of the grain pattern of the boards, use a clear or tinted varnish, or a stain followed by

1 Use a floor sander to smooth and strip old floorboards. Drape the power cord over one shoulder and raise the drum before starting the machine up.

a varnish. Brush stain on to two or three boards at a time, keeping a wet edge so that any differences in shade will be less noticeable. Brush on three coats of varnish, thinning the first with 10 per cent white spirit (paint thinner), and allowing six hours between coats. Keep the room well ventilated.

TIPS

Sanding creates lots of dust, so wear a facemask and goggles. When sanding, raise the drum at the end of each pass to prevent damage to the boards while the machine is stationary. For safety, drape the power cord of the sander over one shoulder.

2 Run the machine at 45 degrees to the board direction to start with, first in one direction, then in the other, at right angles to the original passes made.

3 Then switch to a medium-grade abrasive and run the sander back and forth, parallel to the board direction. Finish off with fine-grade abrasive.

4 Use a smaller disc or belt sander to strip areas close to the skirtings (baseboards) and door thresholds.

5 Use a scraper to remove paint or varnish from inaccessible areas such as around pipework, then sand the stripped wood smooth by hand.

LAYING WOODSTRIP FLOORING

Woodstrip flooring is available in two main types: as solid planks, and as laminated strips (rather like plywood) with a decorative surface veneer. Lengths range from as little as 400mm (16in) up to 1.8m (6ft), and widths from 70mm (2¾in) up to around 200mm (8in). Solid planks are usually about 15mm (⅝in) thick; laminated types are a little thinner.

Both types are generally tongued-and-grooved on their long edges for easy fitting. Some are designed to be fixed to a wooden sub-floor by secret nailing; others are loose-laid, using clips to hold the strips together. Laminated strips are generally pre-finished; solid types may also be, but some need sealing once they have been laid.

All the hard work involved in putting down woodstrip flooring lies in the preparation; the actual laying, like so many decorating jobs, is simple.

Always unpack the strips and leave them in the room where they will be laid for at least seven days to acclimatize to the temperature and humidity levels in the home. This will help to avoid buckling due to expansion, or shrinkage due to contraction, when laid.

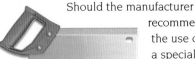

Should the manufacturer recommend the use of a special underlay – which may be plastic sheeting, glass fibre matting or foam – put this down first, taping or stapling the seams together for a smooth finish.

1 Remove the skirtings (baseboards) and make sure that the sub-floor is clean, dry and level. Unroll the special cushioned underlay across the floor, taping one end to keep it in place. Tape or staple the seams together to prevent them from rucking up.

4 The last board is fitted without clips. Cut it to width, allowing for the spacers as in step 2, and apply adhesive along its grooved edge.

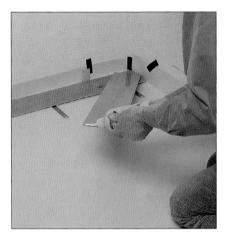

2 Prepare the boards by fitting the joint clips into their grooves. Lay the first length, clips outward, using spacers to create an expansion gap at the wall. Glue the ends of the boards together.

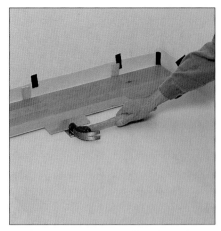

3 Position the second row of boards, tapping them together with a hammer and an offcut so that the clips on the first row engage in the groove of the second. Stagger the boards so that the joints don't coincide with those of adjacent rows.

5 Insert some protective packing against the wall before levering the strip into place. Tap it down level with a hammer and protect the floor with a board offcut. Replace the skirtings to hide the expansion gaps.

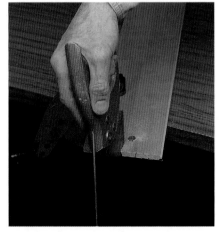

6 To fit a board around a pipe, mark its position and drill a suitably sized hole. Then cut out a tapered wedge, which can be glued back after fitting the board.

LAYING WOOD MOSAIC FLOORING

The least expensive way of creating a decorative timber floor finish is by laying mosaic floor tiles, which are square tiles made from a number of small fingers of decorative hardwood mounted on a cloth or felt backing sheet. This acts as an underlay as well as a means of bonding the fingers together; the result is a sheet that will bend along the joint lines, so it is easily cut to size if required. Alternatively, the fingers may be wired or stuck together to produce a rigid tile. In either case, tiles are generally 300mm (12in) or 450mm (18in) square.

The fingers themselves may be solid wood or veneer on a cheaper softwood backing, and are usually arranged in a basket-weave pattern; however, other patterns are also available. A wide range of wood types is available. Some tiles are supplied sealed; others have to be sealed after being laid.

Laying wood-block floor tiles is a comparatively straightforward job, similar to any other floor tiling project in terms of preparation and setting-out. Store the panels unpacked in the room where they will be laid for at least seven days, to allow them to acclimatize to indoor temperature and humidity levels. This will help to reduce shrinkage or expansion after the tiles are laid. However, an expansion gap should always be left around the perimeter of the room.

1 Work from the centre of the floor outward, stretching strings between the centres of opposite walls to find the starting point. Mark out guidelines and spread some adhesive over a small area of the floor.

4 To cut edge pieces, lay a whole tile over the last whole tile laid and place another on top, butted against the skirting (baseboard). Draw along its edge on the middle tile. Over-cut to allow for the expansion gap.

2 Align the first tile carefully with the tiling guidelines and press it firmly down into the adhesive. Bed it down with a hammer, using a scrap of wood to protect the surface of the panel from the hammer head.

3 Lay the next panel in the same way, butting it up against its neighbour. Wipe off any adhesive from the tile faces immediately, otherwise it will spoil the finish.

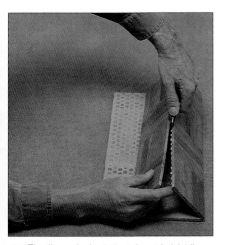

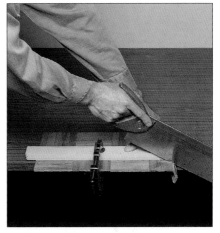

5 The tile can be bent along the main joint lines between the fingers, then sections can be separated by cutting through the backing fabric with a sharp utility knife.

6 More complicated cuts running across the fingers of wood can be made with a tenon saw, using very light pressure to avoid splitting or tearing the thin strips. Sand the edges lightly to remove wood fibres. ▶

7 At door architraves (trims) and other similar obstacles, make a paper template or use a proprietary shape tracer to copy the required shape and mark the tile. Cut along the outline with a coping saw.

8 Cover the cut edges of the tiles by pinning (tacking) lengths of quadrant beading (base shoe) to the skirtings. Alternatively, fit expansion strips cut from cork tiles along the edges to finish.

9 On new work, do not fix the skirtings until the flooring has been laid. They will then hide the expansion gap.

10 Sweep and dust unsealed panels, then apply two or three coats of clear varnish or floor sealer, sanding the surface lightly between coats. Work from the corner farthest away from the door so that you do not become trapped.

PARQUET

Good parquet is a very manageable kind of flooring. There are numerous patterns to be made by combining these wooden blocks. A good trick is to work out the pattern starting from the centre and making it as big a perfect square as you can; then lay a simple border to accommodate all the tricky outside edges. Parquet is often made in oak, but you could dye it with stain or varnish for a richer effect.

TOP RIGHT: You can make up lots of different patterns. The example here would be easy to do.

RIGHT: Classic herringbone presents problems at the edges if the room is not perfectly square, but it can be combined with a simpler pattern around the outside.

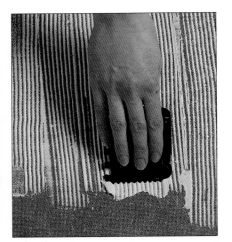

1 Make sure that your floor surface is clean, dry and level. Find your starting point as for laying wood mosaic flooring and draw guidelines on the floor. Using a ridged spreader, coat a manageable area of floor in the specified floor adhesive.

2 Apply wood blocks to the adhesive. Use a length of timber laid across the blocks to check that they all lie flush. Repeat until the floor is covered. Seal the floor with two or three coats of varnish, sanding between coats.

LAYING SHEET VINYL

Sheet vinyl flooring can be difficult to lay because it is wide and comparatively stiff, and edge cutting must be done accurately if gaps are not to be noticeable against skirtings (baseboards). Lengths of quadrant beading (base shoe) can be pinned (tacked) around the perimeter of the room to disguise any serious mistakes.

Most rooms contain at least one long straight wall, and it is often easiest to press the vinyl into the angle between wall and floor and cut along it with the knife held at a 45-degree angle. Then press the ends of the length neatly against the walls at right angles to the first wall, make small diagonal cuts at internal and external angles, and trim the edges to fit there.

1 Unless the wall is perfectly straight, make a cut at the corner and trim the adjacent edges of the sheet with a sharp knife along the angle of wall and floor.

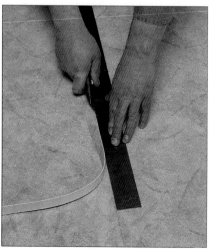

4 To join sheet vinyl edge to edge, overlap the two sheets so that the pattern matches and cut through both layers against a steel straightedge. Discard the waste strips.

5 Place a strip of double-sided adhesive tape underneath the joint line, peel off the backing paper and press the two cut edges firmly down on to the tape.

2 At door architraves (trims), make cuts into the edge of the sheet down to floor level so the sheet will lie flat, and trim off the tongues of excess material.

3 Use a similar technique for trimming the sheet around larger obstacles, such as washbasin pedestals.

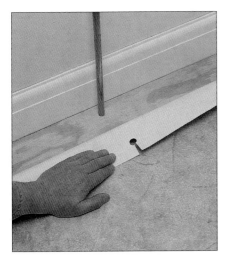

6 To fit the vinyl sheet around pipework, make a cut into it at the pipe position and then trim out a circle of the material to fit around the pipe.

7 At door openings, fit threshold (saddle) strips to anchor the edges of the sheet. Here, an existing strip has been prised up and is being hammered down again to grip the vinyl.

TEMPLATES FOR SHEET VINYL

Where sheet vinyl flooring is being laid around unusually shaped obstacles, such as washbasin pedestals and piping, the best way of obtaining an accurate fit is to make a template of the obstacle so that its shape can be transferred on to the vinyl. Tape together sheets of paper and cut them roughly to the outline of the room and the obstacle. Tape the template to the floor, and use a block of wood and a pencil (or a pair of compasses) to draw a line on the template parallel with the outline of the obstacle. Next, transfer the template to the vinyl, and use the same block of wood or compass setting to scribe lines back on to the vinyl itself. These lines will accurately represent the shape of the room and the obstacle. Cut along them and remove the waste, then stick down edges and seams as before.

A shape tracer, which incorporates a series of adjustable plastic or metal fingers, can also be used to transfer the shapes of obstacles to the vinyl.

1 Use a small block of wood and a pencil to scribe the wall outline on to the paper template laid on the floor.

4 Repeat step 2 to scribe the outline of the obstacle on to the vinyl. Fix the pencil to the block with tape or a rubber band if that makes it easier to use.

PREPARING THE TEMPLATE

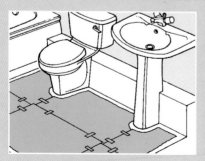

To make a cutting template for a room full of obstacles, such as a bathroom, tape sheets of paper together with their edges about 50mm (2in) from the room walls all around. Tear in from the edges to fit the template around the obstacles as shown, ready for the outline of the room and the obstacles to be scribed on to the template with a block of wood and a pencil.

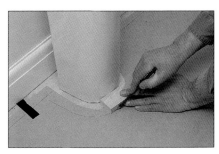

2 Tape the template over the sheet vinyl and use the same block with a pencil to scribe a copy of the room outline back on to the vinyl.

3 Use the same scribing technique to transfer the outline of obstacles such as washbasin pedestals on to the paper template.

5 Using a sharp utility knife, cut carefully around the outline of the obstacle. Make a cut into the waste area, test the cut-out for fit, and trim it slightly if necessary.

6 To make cut-outs around pipes, use a slim block and a pencil to scribe the pipe position on to the template as four lines at right angles to each other.

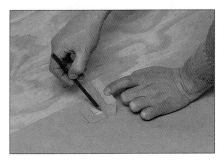

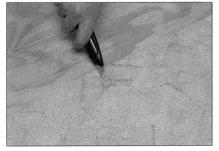

7 Place the template over the vinyl at the pipe position, and use the same block and pencil to mark the cut-out on the vinyl as a small square.

8 Use compasses or a pipe offcut to draw a circle inside the square, then cut around the circle and into the waste area from the edge.

VINYL, LINO AND CORK FLOOR TILES

Vinyl, lino and cork floor tiles are available in both plain and self-adhesive types. Cork tiles may be unsealed or vinyl-coated. For plain vinyl tiles, an emulsion-type latex flooring adhesive is used, while plain cork tiles and lino tiles are best stuck with a water-based contact adhesive. For vinyl-coated cork tiles, use a special vinyl acrylic adhesive.

Since these tiles are comparatively thin, any unevenness in the sub-floor will show through the tiles. Cover wooden floors with a hardboard underlay first. Concrete floors may need localized repairs or treatment with a self-smoothing compound.

Set the floor out carefully. Find the centre-point of the floor by linking the midpoints of opposite pairs of walls with string lines. Dry-lay rows of tiles to see how many whole tiles will fit, move the rows if necessary, then chalk the string lines to mark the starting point.

1 If using self-adhesive tiles, simply peel the backing paper off and place the tile in position on the sub-floor against marked guidelines.

2 Align self-adhesive tiles carefully before sticking them down; the adhesive grabs positively and repositioning may be difficult.

3 If using non-adhesive tiles, spread the appropriate type of adhesive on the sub-floor, using a notched spreader to ensure that an even thickness is applied.

4 After laying an area of tiles, use a smooth block of wood to work along the joins (seams), pressing them down. This will ensure that they are all bedded firmly in the adhesive.

5 At the border, lay a tile over the last tile laid, butt another against the skirting (baseboard) and mark its edge on the tile underneath.

6 Place the marked tile on a board and cut it with a sharp knife. The exposed part of the sandwiched tile in step 5 will fit the gap perfectly.

7 Fit the cut piece of border tile in place. Trim its edge slightly if it is a tight fit. Mark, cut and fit the other border tiles in exactly the same way.

8 At an external corner, lay a whole tile over the last whole tile in one adjacent row, butt another against the wall and draw along its edge.

9 Move the sandwiched tile to the other side of the corner, again butt the second whole tile against the wall and mark its edge on the sandwiched tile.

10 Use the utility knife to cut out the square waste section along the marked lines, and offer up the L-shaped border tile to check its fit before fixing it.

LAYING FOAM-BACKED CARPET

Laying traditional woven carpet can be difficult for the amateur, because if it is to wear well it has to be correctly tensioned across the room by using gripper strips and a carpet stretcher. However, there is no reason why the do-it-yourselfer should not lay less expensive foam-backed carpet in, for example, a spare bedroom. It is possible to disguise any slight inaccuracies that creep into the cutting and fitting process more easily here than with a sheet vinyl floor covering.

Start by putting a paper or cloth underlay on the floor, taping the seams and stapling the underlay in place so that it cannot creep as work continues. Unroll the carpet across the room, with the excess lapping up the walls. Roughly trim the excess all around the room, leaving 50mm (2in) for final trimming. Make small cuts at external corners, such as around chimney breasts (fireplace projections), and let the tongues fall back into the alcoves, then trim off the waste across the face of the chimney breast. Next, press the carpet into internal corners and mark the corner point with a finger. Make cuts to remove the triangle of carpet from the internal angle. Finally, trim the perimeter with a knife drawn along the angle between skirting (baseboard) and wall, and secure the edges with double-sided adhesive tape. Fit threshold (saddle) strips across door openings.

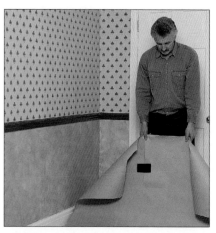

1 Before laying a foam-backed carpet, put down a paper or cloth underlay to keep the foam from sticking to the floor. Tape the seams and staple it in place to prevent it from creeping and rucking up as you work.

4 Work the carpet across the floor to the opposite wall to ensure that it is laying flat. Then trim that edge against the skirting (baseboard) and tape it down too.

2 Put double-sided adhesive tape all around the perimeter of the room, then unroll the carpet and position it so that it laps up the room walls.

3 Butt the edge of the carpet against the longest straight wall in the room. Peel the backing paper off the adhesive tape and press the edge of the carpet into place, working along the wall from one end to the other.

5 Make cuts at internal and external corners to bed the carpet on to the tape. Trim excess carpet by drawing a knife along the angle. Take care not to over-trim.

6 Use adhesive seaming tape to join sections of carpet together where necessary in particularly large rooms. Pressure from a wallpaper seam roller ensures a good bond with the tape, preventing the edges from lifting.

LAYING WOVEN CARPET

The laying and trimming technique used for fitting woven carpets is broadly similar to that described for foam-backed carpets, with two main exceptions: the edges are secured on toothed gripper strips instead of by double-sided adhesive tape, and the carpet must be tensioned across the room to ensure that it wears evenly and cannot ruck up in use.

Start by nailing the gripper strips to the floor all around the room, using a hardboard or cardboard spacer to set them about 10mm (⅜in) away from the skirtings (baseboards). Then put down a good-quality foam underlay, paper side up, cutting it to fit just inside the gripper strips. Tape any seams and staple the underlay to the floor at regular intervals.

Now unroll the carpet, trim it roughly and make small diagonal cuts at internal and external corners. Use a carpet fitter's bolster or a clean brick bolster (stonecutter's chisel) to press one edge of the carpet down on to the gripper strips, then trim off excess carpet and use the bolster to tuck the carpet edge into the gap between the strips and the wall.

Use the carpet stretcher to tension the carpet along the adjacent walls and across the room, hooking it on to the gripper strips as each section is stretched. Trim along the other walls too, and fit the carpet neatly into the doorway, securing it with a threshold (saddle) strip.

1 Nail gripper strips around the perimeter of the room, using a spacer to set them slightly away from the skirting (baseboard). The edge of the carpet will be tucked into the gap.

4 Press one edge of the carpet on to the gripper strips with a carpet fitter's bolster to ensure that the angled teeth are able to grip the carpet backing securely.

2 Lay underlay, trimmed to butt up to the gripper strips. Tape pieces together as necessary, then staple the underlay to the floor at regular intervals.

3 Unroll the carpet and trim it roughly all around. Then make cuts at external corners so that tongues of carpet will fit around them.

5 Cut off the excess carpet along this edge by running a sharp utility knife along the angle between the gripper strip and the skirting, as shown. Take care not to damage the skirting with the knife by holding the blade at an angle away from it.

6 Use the blade of the bolster to tuck the trimmed edge of the carpet into the angle between the gripper strip and the skirting. Then tension the carpet along adjacent walls with the carpet stretcher. Attach the carpet to the gripper strips in the same manner. ▶

7 Make release cuts at all the internal corners, then trim the waste carpet along the other walls of the room as before and tuck the cut edges into the perimeter gaps. This will provide a neat finish to the edges of the carpet.

8 At door frames and similar obstacles, trim the carpet to follow the contours of the obstacle as closely as possible, and press it on to the gripper strips.

STRETCHING CARPET

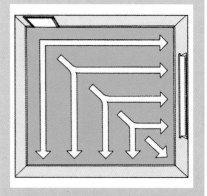

9 Complete the installation by fitting a door threshold (saddle) strip. Different types are available for linking carpet to carpet, and carpet to smooth floor coverings.

Stretch a carpet along two adjacent walls of the room, hooking it on to the gripper strips. Then stretch it across the room, first in one direction, then in the other.

LAYING STAIR CARPET

The technique of carpeting a flight of stairs is similar in principle to that used for carpeting a room, with gripper strips being used to hold the carpet securely to the treads. The job is easiest on a straight flight, but it is not too difficult to cope with winding flights or projecting bullnose steps because cuts can be made across the carpet at any point on the flight and the seams hidden neatly at the back of the tread.

Start by nailing on the gripper strips, just above the bottom edge of each riser and just in front of the rear edge of each tread. The space between them should be about the same as the thickness of a single fold of the carpet. Instead of two lengths of the normal plywood-based strip, special one-piece L-section metal grippers can be used here. Add short lengths of ordinary gripper strip to the sides of the treads,

just less than the thickness of the carpet away from the sides of the flight. Next, cut pieces of underlay to cover each tread and the face of the riser below, and fix them in position with the aid of a staple gun or carpet tacks.

Start laying the carpet at the top of the flight of stairs. If the same carpet is being used on the landing, this should be brought over the edge of the top step and down the face of the first riser. If you do this, the top edge of the stair carpet should be tucked into the gripper strips at the bottom of the first riser. Trim the edges of the carpet on the first tread, then on the next riser, and tuck them in before locking the fold of carpet into the gripper strips at the back of the next tread with a carpet fitter's bolster. Continue in this way to the bottom of the flight, where the stair carpet always finishes at the base of the last riser, whether or not the floor below is covered with the same carpet.

1 Cut lengths of carpet gripper strip to fit across the width of the flight, and nail them in position at the foot of each riser and also at the back of each tread.

2 Next, cut and fit a short length of gripper strip to the sides of each tread. Position them just less than the carpet thickness away from the sides of the flight. ▶

3 Cut underlay to fit adjacent treads and risers, and tack them in place so that they fit smoothly over the nosing at the front of the tread.

4 As an alternative to using two lengths of plywood gripper strip in the tread/riser angle, fit a one-piece L-section metal strip.

5 Begin fitting the carpet at the top of the flight, trimming each tread and riser in turn, then forcing a fold of carpet into the angled gripper strips.

6 On an open-string staircase, either trim the carpet to fit around each baluster or fold over the edge and tack it to fit against the baluster, as shown here.

7 On winder (curved) stairs, cut carpet to cover each tread and the riser below. Align the weave at right angles to the riser.

8 Secure each piece of carpet to the gripper strip at the rear of the tread first, then stretch it over the tread and down to the next gripper strip.

9 Trim off the waste from the bottom edge of the riser and tuck in the carpet at the sides. Repeat the cutting and fitting sequence for any other winder steps on the flight.

10 If the flight finishes with a projecting bullnose step, trim and tack the carpet to the riser, as shown, and cover the riser with a separate strip.

ALTERNATIVE FIXINGS

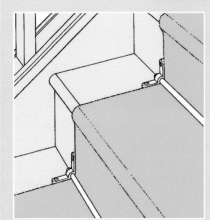

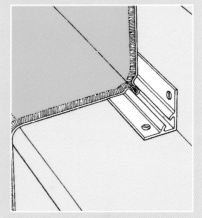

ABOVE: When laying a stair runner rather than a full-width carpet, paint or stain the stair treads and anchor the runner in place with stair rods.

ABOVE: If you are using foam-backed carpet on your stairs, fit special gripper strips for foam-backed carpet into the angles between treads and risers.

FLOORING VARIATIONS

In years gone by, people wanted floors to
last a lifetime. Today we change our
furnishings – and our homes – more often,
so the need is for chic, inexpensive flooring
with instant design impact. If in doubt about
a room's final use or colour scheme, a
beautiful neutral floor will allow you to alter
either. The scale of a room is also important:
large patterns are seen to best advantage
only in large rooms with the minimum of
furniture. However, floors are often the main
feature of halls and passages, even more so
when seen from an upper landing. In this
situation, go for a really eye-catching
treatment. The following pages will give
you a taste of what is possible with the
application of a little imagination.

DISTRESSED FLOORBOARDS

Wooden floors are often appealing because of their subtle variations of colour, which improve with age. Your wooden floors may not be in a great state to begin with, though, or may look uninteresting, and you don't really want to wait for the years to work their magic naturally. Wood stains can help to imitate that look in only a few hours. You can create the look of driftwood, weathered teak or other hardwood decking, as found in beach houses. All you need is three different dyes and a thin wash of white emulsion (latex) paint. This technique would give a bleached effect to any wood stain; for example, over a warm mahogany, a wash of cream or white instantly gives the faded look of maturity.

1 First prepare the surface by knocking in any protruding floorboard nails with a nail punch, and removing any old paint spills with a sander.

4 With either a lint-free cloth or a brush, apply the stain. This will colour anything porous, so protect your hands with rubber gloves and wear old clothes.

7 While the stain is still wet, brush on a wash of the diluted white or cream emulsion (latex) paint, about one part emulsion to four parts water.

2 Brush the boards with a wire brush, along the direction of the grain, with the occasional cross stroke to give a distressed effect.

3 Experiment with the stains, mixing colours together – a little should go a long way. Use scrap wood to test the effect.

5 Apply a generous quantity of stain, but rub off the surplus. For an even finish, complete in one session, keeping the joins (seams) between areas random and avoiding overlapping bands of stain.

6 It's better to apply one thin coat all over, then go back and add further coats, perhaps working the stain into knots or grooves with a brush, to give an uneven, weathered look.

8 Using a dry cloth, rub off surplus paint or apply more until you have achieved the effect you want.

9 Seal the finish by applying two coats of clear varnish, brushing along the grain and sanding very lightly between coats.

WOOD-GRAIN CHEQUERBOARD

Painted chequerboards are a recurrent theme for flooring, yet they are rarely seen in natural wood. If you are starting from a concrete or wooden floor, have the new floor covering cut into squares of the size you want, and either screw them in place or stick them down. If your floor is already covered in sheets of plywood or hardboard, mark out a chequerboard pattern, ignoring the natural joins (seams). Wood-graining doesn't have to be done painstakingly carefully; you can alter the effect produced in oil paint until it starts to dry.

Obtain some reference for the wood effect; oak was the inspiration here. The grain effects resemble the wood treated in different ways, half "polished" and half "rough-sawn and sand-blasted". You could also use two different wood effects, such as walnut and maple.

1 Mark out the floor, edging alternate squares with masking tape. Paint them with two shades of cream.

4 After a few minutes, drag a dry graining brush over the finish, to give the grain effect.

7 Then repeat step 4, using a graining comb rather than a dry graining brush, so the grain looks wider.

2 Mix oil colours into an oil-based glaze, to match the wood reference. Thin the result with white spirit (paint thinner), if necessary.

3 For the "lighter" squares, brush the glaze in the direction of the "grain", leaving brush marks. Add cross-hatched strokes.

5 Using a darker oil paint and a fine artist's brush, gently draw in the chevrons of the wood grain.

6 Soften with a brush, adding white spirit if the paint has dried. Allow to dry. For the "darker" squares, repeat step 1.

8 Paint on more noticeable chevrons in the same way, following the grain.

9 Soften the effect, using the graining comb before the brush. Allow to dry. Apply two coats of satin varnish and allow to dry. If you like, burnish with a little non-slip polish.

LINOLEUM IN 3-D PATTERNS

Linoleum now comes in many thicknesses, colours and patterns, and by cutting it into *trompe l'oeil* patterns and playing with slight colour variations, you can create quite grand effects. Lino is hard-wearing, water-resistant and relatively inexpensive and, given this dramatic treatment, reminiscent of the optical effects in the drawings of Escher, it can become the centrepiece of any hall, kitchen or bathroom. Rolls of lino and floor adhesive were used in this project but you could also use self-glued tiles to make a floor reminiscent of a Venetian palazzo.

Before you begin, draw a plan of the design on squared paper and transfer this to the floor by laying out grid lines. To provide a means of cutting the linoleum to shape, make hardboard templates and cut around them with a sharp knife. Take great care to make your cuts accurate, otherwise you will be left with unsightly gaps between the pieces, which will collect dirt.

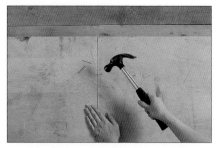

1 You need a smooth, flat surface on which to apply the lino. If necessary, lay a plywood or hardboard floor.

4 Draw grid lines on the floor to act as a guide when laying the lino shapes.

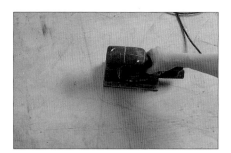

2 Having made sure no nail heads are exposed, lightly sand the floor, to make sure that it is perfectly flat.

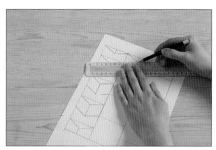

3 Measure the floor. To ensure a good fit, it is very important to work out your pattern on paper first.

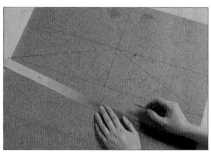

5 Draw each of the pattern shapes on to a sheet of hardboard and cut them out carefully with a saw.

6 Use the templates to cut out the lino shapes. Remember that lino isn't very forgiving and accuracy is all-important.

7 Try out your pattern in pieces of lino to see if any need trimming. If necessary, number them on the back to help you fit them together.

8 Apply contact adhesive to the floor and the backs of the tiles, then carefully fit them in place; you cannot adjust them once they are laid.

PATTERNS WITH CARPET TILES

Carpet tiles are among the simplest of floor coverings to lay, because they are highly tolerant of any slight inaccuracy in cutting to fit. The cheapest types are usually plain in colour and have a very short pile or a corded appearance, while more expensive tiles may have a longer pile and are available in patterns as well as plain colours. Most are designed to be loose-laid, with just the edges secured with bands of adhesive or double-sided tape. This makes it easy to lift individual tiles for cleaning or to even out wear.

Most carpet tiles are marked on the back with an arrow to indicate the pile direction. Align these for a plain effect, or lay them at right angles to create a chequerboard effect. When satisfied with the layout, lift perimeter tiles and put down double-sided tape all around the room. Peel the backing paper off the top of the tape and press the tiles into place. Finish doorways with threshold (saddle) strips.

Another possibility with carpet tiles is to make eye-catching patterns by choosing a selection of different coloured tiles and cutting them into a variety of shapes. Plan the design on paper first and do not start cutting the tiles until you are completely happy with it. If you need to cut very small pieces, make sure all of them are secured with double-sided tape.

1 Measure your room and make sure that the floor is level and all protruding floorboard nails have been driven in.

4 With a steel straightedge and a rigid-bladed knife, score along the marked lines. Don't attempt to cut the tile through in one action.

7 Stick the cut tiles in place, making sure not to pack them too tightly. In this case, the chequered border was laid first, followed by the central pattern. Tread the tiles down.

2 Plan your design on paper. Most rooms are not perfectly square or rectangular, so leave room for an area of plain tiles to edge the pattern.

3 Measure the tiles to work out how many will be needed. Draw the pattern on the backs of the tiles.

5 Starting at the top of the tile, cut down the scored lines. Do this on a solid surface and take great care in doing it.

6 Lay carpet tape and remove the backing. Cut all the tiles for one complete run and fit them, rather than laying little bits at a time.

HIGH-TECH RUBBER FLOORING

Available from specialist rubber manufacturers, rubber mats are valued for their non-slip and protective qualities, and, since they are waterproof, they are particularly useful in, say, a shower room. Rubber is sold from the roll in a broad spectrum of colours, widths and textures. In addition, it doesn't fray and will happily absorb any lumps or strange joins (seams) in a floor. To keep it looking good, clean and seal with a silicone spray polish.

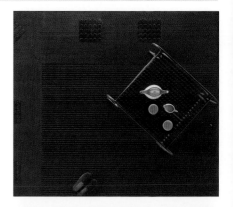

1 Rubber matting in two different designs and rubber tiles have been used here. Measure the floor and the rubber matting, then carefully trim the long runners for the border to size.

2 For each corner, cut a square from the same matting. Divide diagonally and fit them so that the grooves run at right angles to the grooves in the runners. Place the long runners between them.

3 Lay the second matting for the central area. Cut this second type into squares, then cut holes in the runners at regular intervals for them.

4 Secure all the pieces with rubber adhesive, applied to both surfaces. Spray with silicone polish and buff lightly.

CHEQUERBOARD CARPET TILES

Floor mats are easy and cheap to come by, and you can often cut them without the edges fraying. They come in many finishes, some even incorporating words or pictures, and all in manageable rectangles. When these very textured grey polypropylene mats are arranged with the pile running in different directions, a chequerboard effect is achieved. Alternatively, a variety of colours could be used to make an eye-catching pattern.

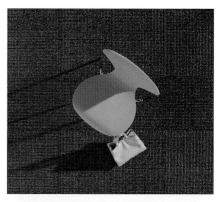

1 Use strings to find the room's centre, and mark with a cross. Measure the floor and work out how many mats you will need. Mark the cuts with a white crayon or chalk on the reverse of the mats.

2 If the mats are of carpet quality, score along the lines with the craft knife, working from the back of the mat. Then cut the mats to size.

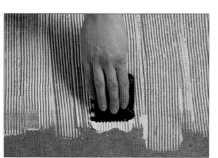

3 Using a notched spreader, apply floor adhesive to the floor, working on a small area at a time.

4 Starting at the centre, carefully lay the mats in position, remembering that, for the effect shown here, you need to alternate the weaves.

INDEX

The publisher would like to thank the following manufacturers for supplying pictures: The Amtico Company 1tr, 11t; Crossley 1bl, 8tr, 12t; Forbo Nairn Ltd 4tl, 7t, 11bl; Heuga 13t; Junckers Ltd 2ml, br, 8b, 15t, b; Kosset 7b, 12b; Mr Tomkinson 14t; Wicanders 8tl, 14b.